WISE QUOTES: FRIEDRICH NIETZSCHE

(143 FRIEDRICH NIETZCHE QUOTES)

Rowan Stevens

A bad conscience is easier to cope with than a bad reputation.

A moral system valid for all is basically immoral.

A politician divides mankind into two classes: tools and enemies.

A subject for a great poet would be God's boredom after the seventh day of creation.

A thought comes when it will, not when I will.

All great things must first wear terrifying and monstrous masks in order to inscribe themselves on the hearts of humanity.

And those who were seen dancing were thought to be insane by those who could not hear the music.

Anyone who has declared someone else to be an idiot, a bad apple, is annoyed when it turns out in the end that he isn't.

As long as you still experience the stars as something above you, you lack the eye of knowledge.

At a certain place in Beethoven's Ninth Symphony, for example, he might feel that he is floating above the earth in a starry dome, with the dream of immortality in his heart; all the stars seem to glimmer around him, and the earth seems to sink ever deeper downwards.

Be careful when you cast out your demons that you don't throw away the best of yourself.

Christianity gave Eros poison to drink; he did not die of it, certainly, but degenerated to Vice.

Close beside my knowledge lies my black ignorance.

Cynicism is the only form in which base souls approach honesty.

Even the most beautiful scenery is no longer assured of our love after we have lived in it for three months, and some distant coast attracts our avarice: possessions are generally diminished by possession.

Every attainment, every step forward in knowledge, follows from courage, from hardness against oneself, from cleanliness in relation to oneself.

Every deep thinker is more afraid of being understood than of being misunderstood.

Every true faith is infallible. It performs what the believing person hopes to find in it. But it does not offer the least support for the establishing of an objective truth. Here the ways of men divide. If you want to achieve peace of mind and happiness, have faith. If you want to be a disciple of truth, then search.

Everyone who has ever built anywhere a new heaven first found the power thereto in his own hell.

From which stars have we fallen to meet each other here?

He who cannot put his thoughts on ice should not enter into the heat of dispute.

He who climbs upon the highest mountains laughs at all tragedies, real or imaginary.

He who despises himself esteems himself as a self-despiser.

He who fights with monsters might take care lest he thereby become a monster. And if you gaze for long into an abyss, the abyss gazes also into you.

He who has a why to live for can bear almost any how.

He who obeys, does not listen to himself!

How much truth can a spirit bear, how much truth can a spirit dare? ... that became for me more and more the real measure of value.

I am a forest, and a night of dark trees: but he who is not afraid of my darkness, will find banks full of roses under my cypresses.

I am no man, I am dynamite.

I am one thing, my writings are another.

I cannot believe in a God who wants to be praised all the time.

I change too quickly: my today refutes my yesterday. When I ascend I often jump over steps, and no step forgives me that.

I fear you close by; I love you far away.

I hate who steals my solitude, without really offer me in exchange company.

I hate you most because you attract, but are not strong enough to pull me to you.

I have forgotten my umbrella.

I have learned to walk: since then I have run. I have learned to fly: since then I do not have to be pushed in order to move.

Now I am nimble, now I fly, now I see myself under myself, now a god dances within me.

I know my fate. One day my name will be associated with the memory of something tremendous — a crisis without equal on earth, the most profound collision of conscience, a decision that was conjured up against everything that had been believed, demanded, hallowed so far.

I love him who seeks to create over and beyond himself and thus perishes.

I mistrust all systematizers and avoid them. the will to a system is a lack of integrity.

I obviously do everything to be hard to understand myself.

I want to learn more and more to see as beautiful what is necessary in things; then I shall be one of those who make things beautiful. Amor fati: let that be my love henceforth! I do not want to wage war against what is ugly. I do not want to accuse; I do not even want to accuse those who accuse. Looking away shall be my only negation. And all in all and on the whole: some day I wish to be only a Yes-sayer.

I would only believe in a god who could dance.

I'm not upset that you lied to me, I'm upset that from now on I can't believe you.

If a man has character, he has also his typical experience, which always recurs.

If you are unwilling to endure your own suffering even for an hour, and continually forestall all possible misfortune, if you regard as deserving of annihilation, any suffering and pain generally as evil, as detestable, and as blots on existence, well, you have then, besides your religion of compassion, yet another religion in your heart (and this is perhaps the mother of the former)-the religion of smug ease. Ah, how little you know of the happiness of man, you comfortable and good-natured ones! For happiness and misfortune are brother and sister, and twins, who grow tall together, or, as with you, remain small together!

In Christianity neither morality nor religion come into contact with reality at any point.

In heaven, all the interesting people are missing.

In individuals, insanity is rare; but in groups, parties, nations and epochs, it is the rule.

In loneliness, the lonely one eats himself; in a crowd, the many eat him. Now choose.

In music the passions enjoy themselves.

In the end things must be as they are and have always been--the great things remain for the great, the abysses for the profound, the delicacies and thrills for the refined, and, to sum up shortly, everything rare for the rare.

In the mountains of truth, you never climb in vain.

Is man merely a mistake of God's? Or God merely a mistake of man.

It is a self-deception of philosophers and moralists to imagine that they escape decadence by opposing it. That is beyond their will; and, however little they acknowledge it, one later discovers that they were among the most powerful promoters of decadence.

It is hard enough to remember my opinions, without also remembering my reasons for them!

It is impossible to suffer without making someone pay for it; every complaint already contains revenge.

It is nobler to declare oneself wrong than to insist on being right --especially when one is right.

It is not a lack of love, but a lack of friendship that makes unhappy marriages.

It is not when truth is dirty, but when it is shallow, that the lover of knowledge is reluctant to step into its waters.

It is the business of the very few to be independent; it is a privilege of the strong. And whoever attempts it, even with the best right, but without being OBLIGED to do so, proves that he is probably not only strong, but also daring beyond measure. He enters into a labyrinth, he multiplies a thousandfold the dangers which life in itself already brings with it; not the least of which is that no one can see how and where he loses his way, becomes isolated, and is torn piecemeal by some minotaur of conscience. Supposing such a one comes to grief, it is so far from the comprehension of men that they neither feel it, nor sympathize with it. And he cannot any longer go back! He cannot even go back again to the sympathy of men!

Live dangerously.

Living in a constant chase after gain compels people to expend their spirit to the point of exhaustion in continual pretense and overreaching and anticipating other. Virtue has come to consist of doing something in less time that someone else. Hours in which honesty is permitted have become rare, and when they arrive one is tired and does not only want to let oneself go but actually wishes to stretch out as long and wide and ungainly as one happens to be... Soon we may well reach the point where people can no longer give in to the desire for a vita contemplativa (that is, taking a walk with ideas and friends) without self-contempt and a bad conscience.

Love brings to light a lover's noble and hidden qualities- his rare and exceptional traits: it is thus liable to be deceptive of his normal qualities.

Love is blind. Friendship closes its eyes.

Love, too, has to be learned.

Man is the cruelest animal.

Man's maturity: to have regained the seriousness that he had as a child at play.

Marriage as a long conversation. - When marrying you should ask yourself this question: do you believe you are going to enjoy talking with this woman into your old age? Everything else in a marriage is transitory, but most of the time that you're together will be devoted to conversation.

Morality is the herd-instinct in the individual.

No one can construct for you the bridge upon which precisely you must cross the stream of life, no one but you yourself alone.

Of all that is written, I love only what a person hath written with his blood. Write with blood, and thou wilt find that blood is spirit.
It is no easy task to understand unfamiliar blood; I hate the reading idlers.
He who knoweth the reader, doeth nothing more for the reader. Another century of readers--and spirit itself will stink.

Every one being allowed to learn to read, ruineth in the long run not only writing but also thinking. Once spirit was God, then it became man, and now it even becometh populace.
He that writeth in blood and proverbs doth not want to be read, but learnt by heart.
In the mountains the shortest way is from peak to peak, but for that route thou must have long legs. Proverbs should be peaks, and those spoken to should be big and tall.
The atmosphere rare and pure, danger near and the spirit full of a joyful wickedness: thus are things well matched.

I want to have goblins about me, for I am courageous. The courage which scareth away ghosts, createth for itself goblins--it wanteth to laugh.

One does not only wish to be understood when one writes; one wishes just as surely not to be understood.

One has to take a somewhat bold and dangerous line with this existence: especially as, whatever happens, we are bound to lose it.

One is fruitful only at the cost of being rich in contradictions.

One loves ultimately one's desires, not the thing desired.

One must not let oneself be misled: they say 'Judge not!' but they send to Hell everything that stands in their way.

One should die proudly when it is no longer possible to live proudly.

Only sick music makes money today.

Pardon me, my friends, I have ventured to paint my happiness on the wall.

Plato was a bore.

Poets are shameless with their experiences: they exploit them.

Sometimes people don't want to hear the truth because they don't want their illusions destroyed.

That which does not kill us makes us stronger.

The advantage of a bad memory is that one enjoys several times the same good things for the first time.

The author must keep his mouth shut when his work startsto speak.

The Christian resolution to find the world ugly and bad has made the world ugly and bad.

The desire to annoy no one, to harm no one, can equally well be the sign of a just as of an anxious disposition.

The earth has a skin and that skin has diseases; one of its diseases is called man.

The essence of all beautiful art, all great art, is gratitude.

The Great Man... is colder, harder, less hesitating, and without fear of 'opinion'; he lacks the virtues that accompany respect and 'respectability,' and altogether everything that is the 'virtue of the herd.' If he cannot lead, he goes alone... He knows he is incommunicable: he finds it tasteless to be familiar... When not speaking to himself, he wears a mask. There is a solitude within him that is inaccessible to praise or blame.

The heaviest burden: What, if some day or night, a demon were to steal after you into your loneliest loneliness and say to you: 'This life, as you now live it and have lived it, you will have to live once more and innumerable times more; and there will be nothing new in it, but every pain and every joy and every thought and sigh... must return to you—all in the same succession and sequence—even this spider and this moonlight between the trees and even this moment and I myself. The eternal hourglass of existence is turned over again and again—and you with it, speck of dust!' Would you not throw yourself down and gnash your teeth and curse the demon who spoke thus? Or have you once experienced a tremendous moment when you would have answered him: 'You are a god, and never have I heard anything more divine!' If this thought were to gain possession of you, it would change you as you are, or perhaps crush you. The question in each and every thing, do you want this once more and innumerable times more? would lie upon your actions as the greatest weight. Or how well disposed would you have to become to yourself and to life to crave nothing more fervently than this ultimate eternal confirmation and seal?

The individual has always had to struggle to keep from being overwhelmed by the tribe. If you try it, you will be lonely often, and sometimes frightened. But no price is too high to pay for the privilege of owning yourself.

The life of the enemy. Whoever lives for the sake of combating an enemy has an interest in the enemy's staying alive.

The man of knowledge must be able not only to love his enemies but also to hate his friends.

The maturity of man—that means, to have reacquired the seriousness that one had as a child at play

The most spiritual men, as the strongest, find their happiness where others would find their destruction: in the labyrinth, in hardness against themselves and others, in experiments. Their joy is self-conquest: asceticism becomes in them nature, need, and instinct. Difficult tasks are a privilege to them; to play with burdens that crush others, a recreation. Knowledge—a form of asceticism. They are the most venerable kind of man: that does not preclude their being the most cheerful and the kindliest.

The overman...Who has organized the chaos of his passions, given style to his character, and become creative. Aware of life's terrors, he affirms life without resentment.

The pure soul is a pure lie.

The real world is much smaller than the imaginary.

The secret of realizing the greatest fruitfulness and the greatest enjoyment of existence is: to live dangerously! Build your cities on the slopes of Vesuvius! Send your ships out into uncharted seas! Live in conflict with your equals and with yourselves! Be robbers and ravagers as soon as you ca not be rulers and owners, you men of knowledge! The time will soon past when you could be content to live concealed int he woods like timid deer!

The snake which cannot cast its skin has to die. As well the minds which are prevented from changing their opinions; they cease to be mind.

The spiritualization of sensuality is called love: it is a great triumph over Christianity.

The strength of a person's spirit would then be measured by how much 'truth' he could tolerate, or more precisely, to what extent he needs to have it diluted, disguised, sweetened, muted, falsified.

The surest way to corrupt a youth is to instruct him to hold in higher esteem those who think alike than those who think differently.

The text has disappeared under the interpretation.

The thought of suicide is a great consolation: by means of it one gets through many a dark night.

The tree that would grow to heaven must send its roots to hell.

There are no facts, only interpretations.

There is a certain right by which we many deprive a man of life, but none by which we may deprive him of death; this is mere cruelty.

There is always some madness in love. But there is also always some reason in madness.

There is an old illusion. It is called good and evil.

There is no such thing as moral phenomena, but only a moral interpretation of phenomena.

They call you heartless; but you have a heart and I love you for being ashamed to show it.

Thoughts are the shadows of our feelings -- always darker, emptier and simpler.

To learn to see- to accustom the eye to calmness, to patience, and to allow things to come up to it; to defer judgment, and to acquire the habit of approaching and grasping an individual case from all sides. This is the first preparatory schooling of intellectuality. One must not respond immediately to a stimulus; one must acquire a command of the obstructing and isolating instincts.

Truths are illlusions which we have forgotten are illusions.

Two great European narcotics, alcohol and Christianity.

Virtue is under certain circumstances merely an honorable form of stupidity: who could be ill-disposed toward it on that account? And this kind of virtue has not been outlived even today. A kind of sturdy peasant simplicity, which, however, is possible in all classes and can be encountered only with respect and a smile, believes even today that everything is in good hands, namely in the hands of God; and when it maintains this proportion with the same modest certainty as it would that two and two make four, we others certainly refrain from contradicting. Why disturb THIS pure foolishness? Why darken it with our worries about man, people, goal, future? And even if we wanted to do it, we could not. They project their own honorable stupidity and goodness into the heart of things (the old God, deus myops, still lives among them!); we others — we read something else into the heart of things: our own enigmatic nature, our contradictions, our deeper, more painful, more mistrustfulwisdom.

We should consider every day lost on which we have not danced at least once.

What if a demon were to creep after you one night, in your loneliest loneliness, and say, 'This life which you live must be lived by you once again and innumerable times more; and every pain and joy and thought and sigh must come again to you, all in the same sequence. The eternal hourglass will again and again be turned and you with it, dust of the dust!' Would you throw yourself down and gnash your teeth and curse that demon? Or would you answer, 'Never have I heard anything more divine'?

What is great in man is that he is a bridge and not a goal: what is lovable in man is that he is an OVER-GOING and a DOWN-GOING.

What is happening to me happens to all fruits that grow ripe.
It is the honey in my veins that makes my blood thicker, and my soul quieter.

What is the truth, but a lie agreed upon.

What then is truth? A movable host of metaphors, metonymies, and anthropomorphisms: in short, a sum of human relations which have been poetically and rhetorically intensified, transferred, and embellished, and which, after long usage, seem to a people to be fixed, canonical, and binding. Truths are illusions which we have forgotten are illusions — they are metaphors that have become worn out and have been drained of sensuous force.

What was silent in the father speaks in the son, and often I found in the son the unveiled secret of the father.

When we are tired, we are attacked by ideas we conquered long ago.

When you stare into the abyss the abyss stares back at you.

Whoever fights monsters should see to it that in the process he does not become a monster. And if you gaze long enough into an abyss, the abyss will gaze back into you.

Whoever thought that he had understood something of me had merely construed something out of me, after his own image.

Whoever, at any time, has undertaken to build a new heaven has found the strength for it in his own hell...

Without forgetting it is quite impossible to live at all.

Without music, life would be a mistake.

Woman was God's second mistake.

You desire to LIVE according to Nature? Oh, you noble Stoics, what fraud of words! Imagine to yourselves a being like Nature, boundlessly extravagant, boundlessly indifferent, without purpose or consideration, without pity or justice, at once fruitful and barren and uncertain: imagine to yourselves INDIFFERENCE as a power—how COULD you live in accordance with such indifference? To live—is not that just endeavouring to be otherwise than this Nature? Is not living valuing, preferring, being unjust, being limited, endeavouring to be different? And granted that your imperative, living according to Nature, means actually the same as living according to life—how could you do DIFFERENTLY? Why should you make a principle out of what you yourselves are, and must be? In reality, however, it is quite otherwise with you: while you pretend to read with rapture the canon of your law in Nature, you want something quite the contrary, you extraordinary stage-players and self-deluders! In your pride you wish to dictate your morals and ideals to Nature, to Nature herself, and to incorporate them therein; you insist that it shall be Nature according to the Stoa, and would like everything to be made after your own image, as a vast, eternal glorification and generalism of Stoicism! With all your love for truth, you have forced yourselves so long, so persistently, and with such hypnotic rigidity to see Nature FALSELY, that is to say, Stoically, that you are no longer able to see it otherwise—and to crown all, some unfathomable superciliousness gives you the Bedlamite hope that BECAUSE you are able to tyrannize over yourselves—Stoicism is self-tyranny—Nature will also allow herself to be tyrannized over: is not the Stoic a PART of Nature?... But this is an old and everlasting story: what happened in old times with the Stoics still happens today, as soon as ever a philosophy begins to believe in itself. It always creates the world in its own image; it cannot do otherwise; philosophy is this tyrannical impulse itself, the most spiritual Will to

Power, the will to creation of the world, the will to the causaprima.

You have your way. I have my way. As for the right way, the correct way, and the only way, it does not exist.

You know these things as thoughts, but your thoughts are not your experiences, they are an echo and after-effect of your experiences: as when your room trembles when a carriage goes past. I however am sitting in the carriage, and often I am the carriage itself.
In a man who thinks like this, the dichotomy between thinking and feeling, intellect and passion, has really disappeared. He feels his thoughts. He can fall in love with an idea. An idea can make him ill.

You look up when you wish to be exalted. And I look down because I am exalted.

You must have chaos within you to give birth to a dancing star.

You say 'I' and you are proud of this word. But greater than this- although you will not believe in it - is your body and its great intelligence, which does not say 'I' but performs 'I'.

You say, it's dark. And in truth, I did place a cloud before your sun. But do you not see how the edges of the cloud are already glowing and turning light.

Your only problem, perhaps, is that you scream without letting yourself cry.

www.ingramcontent.com/pod-product-compliance
Lightning Source LLC
Chambersburg PA
CBHW071255070526
44583CB00017B/2478